Being Frugal and Saving Money

Saving is a kind of Earning

ABSTRACT

What is saving? Saving is the collection or accumulation of funds that can be used in the future to gain protection from the harsh adversities of life. Saving in the present can help provide flexibility in financial pressures in the future.

By M. Naveed

TABLE OF CONTENTS

All Rights Reserved

Disclaimer

The information in this book is provided for informational purposes only and it is not intended for use as a substitute for proper financial or legal direction by a qualified financial or legal advisor. The information is believed to be accurate as presented based on research by the author.

The author or publisher is not responsible for financial loss or damage incurred by implementing ideas mentioned in this book. The author or publisher is not responsible for errors or omissions that may exist.

Warning

The Book is for informational purposes only and before starting or running any activity or business, it is recommended that you consult with your financial or legal professional. Always follow all laws and regulations mentioned in this book regarding activities, taxes, selling, buying, or ecommerce.

BEING FRUGAL AND SAVING MONEY

INTRODUCTION:

The general perception and attitude of most people living in today's busy lifestyle is that it is socially acceptable to spend most of what you earn. People believe that putting in all the hard work to earn this wealth means it should be spent on enjoyment and making life luxurious. But in practical life this is not true. If you spend all your money without saving for rainy days, you might end up in great trouble. In the short run you might feel happy from all the spending but in the long run saving is the right path to follow. Have you ever thought what might happen if you lost your job tomorrow or God forbid end up in an accident or car crash. Truth is that all our life we encounter various surprises and unforeseen events. And most of the time spending of money in response to them is unavoidable. If you are a saver and have some bucks set aside for such surprises, it will definitely bring about some reduction in the stress and anxiety of not having the money.

What is saving? Saving is the collection or accumulation of funds that can be used in the future to gain protection from the harsh adversities of life. Saving in the present can help provide flexibility in financial pressures in the future.

Since time immemorial we have been told to save money by our parents, teachers, elders, financial experts, friends and colleagues. It is very easy to advise someone to be frugal and save money but in reality it is very difficult. It simply does not mean that you stop overspending, but there is a lot more to it. It is a steep challenge, in which most people fail. But those with the strong determination and control over their desires can surely prove their mark.

Before someone actually decides to start this challenging task, there are many questions that come to mind:

- What are the major and minor areas where money can be saved?
- How much money should be saved?

- Where should this amount be saved?
- How can you stop yourself from spending your savings?

IMPORTANCE OF BEING FRUGAL AND SAVING MONEY:

The question that arises in every person's mind is why save if you can afford to buy whatever you need. Why is then saving such an important act. There are a number of reasons why saving money can be considered a wise decision. Being frugal may be understood by different people differently. Saving money and spending wisely is necessary because every human being goes through different ups and downs of life and as such has different sources of earning money. There are always variations in the incomes and spending patterns of individuals and families. If you do not save for mishaps or unexpected situations, you may have to face severe difficulties and problems in such events. Before actually analyzing various options for saving money let us see why saving money is so important.

A. SAVING FOR EMERGENCY SITUATIONS:

It is the habit of many frugal people to keep aside money on regular basis. They use this money to cover unforeseen events and situations. You can face an unexpected car breakdown requiring maintenance on an urgent basis, or some medical emergency like appendicitis and other unfortunate events like joblessness. The amount of the emergency fund should be enough to bear the basic expenses of the saver for almost three to four months. If you are just planning to start the saving account, you must first analyze your average basic expenses in a month and then start putting the appropriate money aside for this purpose. Additionally for a better support system, you must have good insurance coverage and a financial back up plan designed for such unexpected circumstances.

B. SAVING FOR RETIREMENT BENEFITS:

The second reason why people opt to save money is the concept of job retirement. The earlier you start this process, the less you have to save in the future. By opening a proper retirement fund at some financial institution, the more you save the more you will start earning interest on it. Most salaried job options also have a good pension and retirement plan. But apart from that you should yourself also contribute appropriately to this account.

C. SAVING FOR DOWN PAYMENTS:

Buying property or other consumer items has become quite easy due to installment systems introduced in banks and other financial institutions. However while making the purchase; a nominal down payment is required. If you are a wise saver your savings can help in the provision of this down payment. By inquiring about the down payment of the item like a house beforehand you can start saving the right amount at the right time. It also enhances your negotiation powers while establishing a deal.

D. SAVING FOR VACATIONS AND TRIPS:

Saving can be done for the purpose of enjoying life and making luxury trips to exotic places. By setting up a vacation or holiday account, you can punch in small amounts in it on a regular basis and enjoy your trips with no worries of running short of money. You can plan your trips accounting to the funds you have and vice versa. You can save according to the places you want to visit by estimating the travelling costs, lodging, meals, etc.

E. SAVING FOR A CAR:

Another important necessity in every urban individual's life is having a transportation medium like a car or a motorbike. So, you can start saving. By making an account and adding money to it very soon you'll be able to make the purchase. Once opted to buy, you will be indirectly saving on communication costs. If you have enough cash in hand, you are in better position to negotiate your terms with the dealership. Also this ensures faster delivery.

F. ESTABLISH A SINKING FUND:

A sinking fund is just like an emergency fund where money is continually added and the accumulation of money is used for different purposes. This could be used for car maintenance or home improvements or bearing losses. This will enable you to stop taking money out of the emergency fund because its purpose will be clearer.

G. SAVING FOR EDUCATIONAL PURPOSES:

A very important reason to save money these days is for educational purposes. This could be for self-education or a college fund for your kids. Many people drop out of college or university due to lack of sufficient funds. By collecting money over some time period in an educational fund they can return to pursuing their degree whenever they have saved a sufficient amount of money. It also helps reduce the burden of bearing the expenses of your child's education.

NON-MATERIAL BENEFITS OF SAVING MONEY AND BEING FRUGAL:

Apart from the material benefits, the act of saving also has some non - material or subjective advantages to mankind. These include the following:

A. ENHANCEMENT OF POSITIVE FINANCIAL CHARACTERISTICS:

Being frugal and saving money is a good habit. It improves the well being of individuals by decreasing their financial and economic problems. This habit inculcates the importance of money in our minds. It makes us understand how difficult it is to earn legitimate cash and how easy it is to spend. By putting money aside for unexpected bad days, we also practice an act of discipline by imposing self-accountability and strictness. It will reduce the dependence on credit and debit cards, which are wrongfully established substitutes for cash. They allure us to spend more than we have, thus entrapping us into financial trouble and feeling stressed. However, if we are able to develop a consistent saving attitude in us, we will realize the value of money and how to think before we spend for unnecessary expenses.

B. FINANCIAL FREEDOM AND INDEPENDENCE:

If you are self-sufficient and able to meet your own needs and requirements of unexpected situations, it gives you a sense of achievement and financial independence from others. You do not have to put up with any institution or financial lenders' terms and conditions. You set your own financial goals and schedules and benefit from it.

C. IMPROVEMENT IN SELF CONFIDENCE AND ENDURANCE:

Having money when you need it in unexpected situations gives you a sense of confidence and strength to fight against different odds. It can help you focus on other important things in life rather than small ups and downs that cause mental anxiety or stress. Having a savings account will also ensure that you follow a selected financial plan and do not derail form it from time to time due to minor hiccups. It provides a cushion against the unexpected.

D. REDUCTION IN STRESS LEVELS:

If you are not able to afford all your expenses and face a situation where your earning are less than what you want, you will definitely go for some kind of debt or borrowing. This resort to financial markets may seem like a good choice in the beginning but with passage of time it will become a burden on you and will drain you of all your hard earned income. The piling up of interest can be very stressful and burdensome. So if you have a good savings plan, you might not have to undergo the act of borrowing and your stress levels will be reduced.

E. LESS BORROWING AND MORE WEALTH:

By being frugal and saving appropriately, we can not only reap the psychological benefits but also produce results that reap these subjective benefits. By saving more and borrowing less, we can increase our wealth, which in turn can lead to multiple benefits.

F. WHAT IS BEING FRUGAL AND A FRUGAL WAY OF LIVING?

When we talk about being frugal does it mean we have to be a cheapskate? The answer is no! Frugal living is a smart way of money management. You need to assess how much money you earn and how much is required to meet the bare necessities of life. Over and above calculate what you need with great urgency and what you can do without. That is how you can analyze what you can spend and afford and what is over and above your budget. The key here is to be in-charge of what you have and spend it very wisely.

It requires that you learn to find the best bargain on everything that you purchase. It is like getting the most out of your money reserve. This means that you should shop from thrift houses, garage sales, clearance stores and barter centers to pay the minimum price for the commodity that you want to buy. Use of different discount coupons and other promotional sales discount to reduce the price to the minimum is the key to being frugal.

Another aspect of frugal living is to know when not to shop and when to stop shopping. Not buying something that is not needed on urgent basis or that does not suit your pocket is a wise decision. You should wait with great patience until that thing goes on sale. Frugality is being totally in control of your shopping and spending habits.

It also enables you to use your creativity and abilities to their full capacity. Where you have to hire someone's help, why not do it yourself. Use things that you already have for multi purposes. Using substitutes is also sometimes very effective.

HOW TO SAVE MONEY AND BE FRUGAL:

Some easy methods that help you in adopting a frugal lifestyle and in return save you some money as well are provided below:

A. SAVING MONEY ON FOOD:

The basic necessity of life without which sustenance is impossible is food. It is something that we have to spend on no matter what the circumstances are. But here are some techniques to be frugal and save money on the grocery bill.

1. PANTRY PRINCIPLE:

One should make a list of all the food items that we consume on regular basis. When shopping for those items again, only shop for the same items and with a target of restocking them.

2. AVOID PROCESSED FOOD:

Start cooking frugally. This can be done by cooking everything from raw. Avoid using tinned items or that have been pre packed or processed which are far more expensive. It will not only help you save money also improve your health. The right way is to buy the ingredients for the dish you want to make and prepare it yourself.

3. DO SOME MENU PLANNING:

Based on your eating habits and patterns, devise a menu plan. This can be fortnightly, weekly or monthly. It will definitely save you money when you are not over buying. Buy only the amount that might be required for that menu. No more no less.

4. REDUCE GROCERY STORE TRIPS:

The more you visit the grocery store the more chances there are to overspend. Try not to make frequent visits to grocery stores. Only plan a visit when you have 10 or more things on your list of items to restock.

5.   START YOUR OWN KITCHEN GARDEN:

If you have the space and time, you should definitely save money by starting your own small kitchen garden. Grow whatever you need in it to avoid buying from the market. This is healthy as well as frugal.

6.   SIMPLE EATING:

Keep your eating habit simple and small. Do not emphasize on variety or a large number of dishes. Be a healthy eater. Introduce more and more vegetables and fruits in your diet. Stick to home cooked meals and reduce dependence on ready to eat boxes and already cooked food items.

7.   BULK BUYING:

Many stores offer discounts and rebates on large buys. So go for bulk buying. Buy food items that can last longer and are not perishable. This can save you money through cheaper prices and also by reducing your grocery store trips.

8.   USE BROWN BAGS:

Use brown bags for your lunches. These are considerably less expensive and environmentally friendly.

9.   DO NOT WASTE:

Cook according to your needs. Do not cook in large quantities. Always count the number and portions of meals to be taken.

10. MAKE USE OF LEFTOVERS:

Do not throw away extra quantities or leftovers. Make use of them very wisely.

11. DRINK MORE WATER:

Drink as much water as you can. Water is cheaper and at many places free of cost. Eliminate the use of soft drinks and other flavored beverages and substitute them with water.

12. REDUCE EATING OUT:

You should reduce the number of trips to restaurants and other external eating-places. Rely more on home cooked meals.

13. TAKE YOUR LUNCHBOX:

If you have to go to work or an educational institution, you should take your own home cooked meals with you in a lunch. This will reduce your spending on food stands and lunch items.

14. MAKE YOUR OWN BABY FOOD:

Instead of feeding your baby prepared, tinned or bottled food items, opt instead for homemade baby food. You can find many recipes for wholesome, nutritious baby food on the internet and in books.

B. SAVING ON UTILITIES:

The basic utilities available to all urban or rural households include electricity, gas and telephone service, etc. Using them wisely can save you a bundle on monthly payments. Some of the tips regarding frugality in utility usage are provide below:

1. WATER HEATERS:

In an average household, everyone bathes or takes a shower in the morning before going to work or starting their day. Similarly, use of water increases once everyone returns home in evening. The strategy here is to analyze your water usage patterns and turn the water heater off whenever it is not required.

2. TURN OFF THE TELEVISION:

Whenever not in use, turn your television off. Leaving it on standby consumes energy and drains energy.

3. REUSABLE ITEMS:

Use reusable bags and boxes in the household. Make it a habit. Whether you are going shopping or taking lunch to work, in all instances make use of reusable bags and boxes. They are convenient and long lasting.

4. ADJUST YOUR THERMOSTAT:

According to the temperature on the outside, adjust your heating and cooling thermostat.

5. WEAR WARMER CLOTHES:

If the weather is cold, increase the number layers of clothing, you wear instead of raising the temperature of the heating system. The colder it is the more clothes you should be wearing.

6. TAKE COOL SHOWERS:

In the summers, beat the heat with cool water showers. This would reduce the dependence of air-conditioning. Use of light airy, loose fitting clothing also makes you feel much more comfortable.

7. CLEAN YOUR REFRIGERATOR AND FREEZER:

Keeping your refrigerator and freezer clean can save a lot of electricity. Also making sure that the coil behind the refrigerator is clean is a frugal activity.

8. KEEP YOUR FREEZER FULL:

An empty freezer requires more energy to get cold. So always keep your freezer full. You can use empty milk containers and fill them up with water and stock them in your freezer to keep cool inside. This would require the compressor to come on less.

9. REMOVE ALL UNWANTED ELECTRICITY DRAINS:

Whenever an appliance is left plugged into the electricity socket, it can use up a small amount of electricity. So the key to saving energy is to remove all unused items and appliances from electric sockets. This would definitely bring down the electric bill.

10. LOOK OUT FOR ENERGY DRAINS:

Open windows, doors and other energy leaks in your house can cause your heating or cooling systems to work harder and hence consume more energy. Seal all openings and holes to reduce electricity consumption.

11. USE ONE TELEPHONE MEDIUM:

If you have a cell phone, there is no need to have a landline as well. It will only cost you extra. So get it removed.

12. TURNING OFF SMALL APPLIANCES:

Whenever you leave the room, turn off lights and other electric appliances like fans, television and radios, etc.

13. LEDS AND ENERGY SAVERS:

Instead of tube lights and bulbs try using LEDs and energy savers for light sources. Avoid using lights during daytime and make full use of natural light.

14. PLANT TREES:

Encourage the plantation of shady trees around your house to make it cooler. This reduces temperatures significantly and helps in reduction of electricity bills.

C. HEALTH AND PHYSICAL FITNESS ELEMENTS:

1. DISCONTINUE GYM MEMBERSHIP:

Instead of going to a local gym and paying for use of the facility, create your own DIY home gym in an appropriate place like a basement or lawn.

2. HOME AEROBICS:

Instead of taking costly aerobic classes rent out or buy an aerobics training video or cd to help you learn.

3. HIGH DEDUCTIBLE INSURANCE:

With a healthier family, you should opt for a health care account set aside or an insurance coverage, which is high deductible plan. It needs more out of your pocket expenses before the start of actual insurance cover. The monthly installment is significantly reduced. The money you deposit in the health care account is also non-taxable.

4. QUIT SMOKING:

Smoking is not only a drain on your pocket but also on your health. So quitting smoking can save you a bunch.

5. TAKE EXTRA CARE:

Be cautious of your health and try to live a healthier lifestyle. Be hygienic and protective against germs. Dental health care expenses can also be reduced significantly through proper brushing and cleaning.

D. TRANSPORTATION AND CAR MAINTENANCE:

1. SELF-CHANGE OF OIL:

Learn how to perform general maintenance tasks like oil change of your transport yourself.

2. SHUFFLE YOUR TIRES:

Make sure you rotate your tires on a regular basis. This makes them last longer and save replacement for longer periods.

3. BUY A USED CAR:

Buying a new car is costly but if you opt to buy a used car, you can get a better bargain. There is also more room for negotiating the price of a used car.

4. CAR SHARING:

Instead of using separate cars for all family members, share your car. Plan your schedules beforehand and manage trips and routes accordingly. This will not only prolong the life of the car costs but also save on fuel, maintenance and insurance costs.

5. CAR INSURANCE:

Stick to one insurance company for longer periods and pay an annual insurance premium. This allows discounts and rebates.

6. CARPOOL:

Whether you are going to school, office or the market, use a carpool system. This helps save on transportation expenses.

7. TIRE MAINTENANCE:

Make sure the tires of your car are properly inflated. This will definitely increase their life span.

8. REPLACE AND CLEAN AIRFILTER:

By having a cleaner air filter, you save tremendously on gas consumption. Learn how to clean and change the filter yourself. And do it regularly.

9. GO SLOW:

Speeding and fast driving consumes more gas. So the key is to go slow.

10. PLAN TRIPS TOGETHER:

Plan trips with family and friends to share travelling expenses.

11. WALK:

Wherever and whenever possible use your feet and walk.

E. DRESSING AND SELF-GROOMING:

1. DO YOUR OWN LAUNDRY AND IRONING:

Don't depend on costly laundry services. Wash and iron your own clothes to save money.

2. STICK WITH EXISTING CLOTHES:

If your size changes or there are modifications in fashion, make alterations on existing dresses and save on buying new clothes.

3. BUY ITEMS ON SALE AND AT THRIFT SHOPS:

Always look for clothing on clearance or at end of season sales. You can also browse in a thrift shop and get some good bargains.

4. SHAVING AND CUTTING:

If possible, always shave with a safety razor to save costs on expensive blades. Also learn to cut your own hair.

5. KEEP CHILDREN'S CLOTHES:

If you have more than one kid, don't throw away clothes. They come in handy when the smaller children grow into them.

6. BUY FEWER:

Buy fewer clothing pieces and mix and match them to bring about a unique look. Experiment in creating various styles.

7. CLOTHES SWAPPING:

You can swap your clothes and accessories with friends and family members.

8. HOME REMEDIES:

Instead of buying expensive beauty products and brands, use your kitchen shelves for home remedies and beauty solutions.

F. ENTERTAINMENT:

1. GO OUT:

Plan trips and fun events outdoors such as picnics, park outings and hiking, etc.

2. GAME NIGHTS:

Host and organize game nights with family and friends for great entertainment.

3. LET A FRIEND MAKE DINNER:

Just for a change of taste, you can ask a friend or neighbor make something and you can swap something in return.

4. PLAN YOUR VACATION IN OFF SEASONS:

Do not plan your vacations in peak seasons, as they are more costly.

5. CAMPING TRIPS:

Instead of renting out expensive hotels go for cheaper camping trips and cook your own food.

6. SHARE DVDS AND MOVIES:

Share and exchange movies and books with friends and family.

7. LIBRARY:

Instead of buying a book, go to a library and enjoy reading it for free.

8. GO FOR HEALTHIER HOBBIES:

Take up hobbies like arts and crafts, reading, hiking and bird watching.

G. COMPUTERS AND TECHNICAL EXPENSES:

1. REFILL PRINTER CARTRIDGES:

Always get printer cartridges refilled instead of buying new ones.

2. PRINT IN DRAFT:

Printing in draft mode is an economical way to slash costs.

3. DOWNLOAD FREE SOFTWARE:

Whenever and wherever possible download free software and music from the internet.

4. CONSIDER BUYING REFURBISHED EQUIPMENT:

Instead of buying brand new personal computing equipment you can find refurbished models at better prices.

H. GIFTS AND GIVEAWAYS:

1. HOME-MADE GIFTS:

When giving gifts and presents be creative and provide homemade items.

2. PROVIDE SPECIAL SERVICES:

You can offer to provide special comforting services as gifts.

CONCLUSION:

There are several important reasons why being frugal and saving money is so necessary. Some of these factors are related to our protection and security needs while others are related to our future life and goals. It is simply a wise decision to prepare for the unexpected.

Saving money is vitally important for all kinds of emergent situations. It is not very likely that people will foresee themselves in the middle of a financial crisis, physical disability or health disease or a jobless situation. But fact of the matter is that it happens to a large number of people. In addition to these large scaled problems, smaller issues like car breakdown, medical illnesses, bill payments and unplanned traveling expenses may be better handled by an individual who is saving some money for crisis circumstances. According to experts in this field, any individual who is saving money in an emergency account should at least have enough to meet his basic expenses for at least three months.

Being frugal and saving money is an essential component of future planning. It is the dream of almost all to see their children earn a college or university degree for a better professional prospect. However, due to shortage of funds or financial issues, many such deserving candidates may not even get close to college. Although there are always the options of scholarships or student loan schemes, they might not suffice for all. So it is vitally important to do some saving for your children's brighter future. You should start at an early age, and set aside small amounts in this education account. This will help you provide better for your children. Education may not be the only concern of your parents. It can be a wedding, accommodation, cars or helping your children start a small business. Saving money can help you meet all these requirements.

Although a hard task at first, those who get used it make it a lifestyle. They think frugal and live frugal. Even if you do not face emergencies or social responsibilities, you might save to provide yourself with some entertainment like holidays and vacations like a trip to Disneyland or the Bahamas. You can save for something that you cherish and long for but cannot afford on your monthly income.

Saving money reduces ones reliance on debit and credit cards. Saving accounts earn you interest rather than requiring the payment interest as in the case of borrowing accounts.

Saving is all about managing your financing and activities in a frugal way. You should learn to follow a DIY, do-it-yourself approach to save money on many tasks. Also enhance your creativity and think of out of the box techniques to facilitate the reuse or use of items you already own for multi-purposes. Align your lists of what is needed and what you can live without. Buy quality items. Ensure that what you buy is long lasting and will not cost you heavy amounts on maintenance or replacements. It means that you should be in control of your decisions and desires. Do not let your desires guide you but guide your desires the way you want to.

Mostly you should rely on spending cash and do not engage in overdraft or credit cards just for emergencies. Instead opt to pay yourself first by establishing a savings account and set aside money for unexpected or unplanned expenses. This will save you from mental and physical stress in such emergent situations.

Although it is easier said than done, the benefits of being frugal and saving money are so immense that it makes every person think twice before they spend unnecessarily. It is essentially a self-control and management process that can change the way people plan and think about their future.

PUBLISHER

Gardening Series on Amazon

Health Learning Series

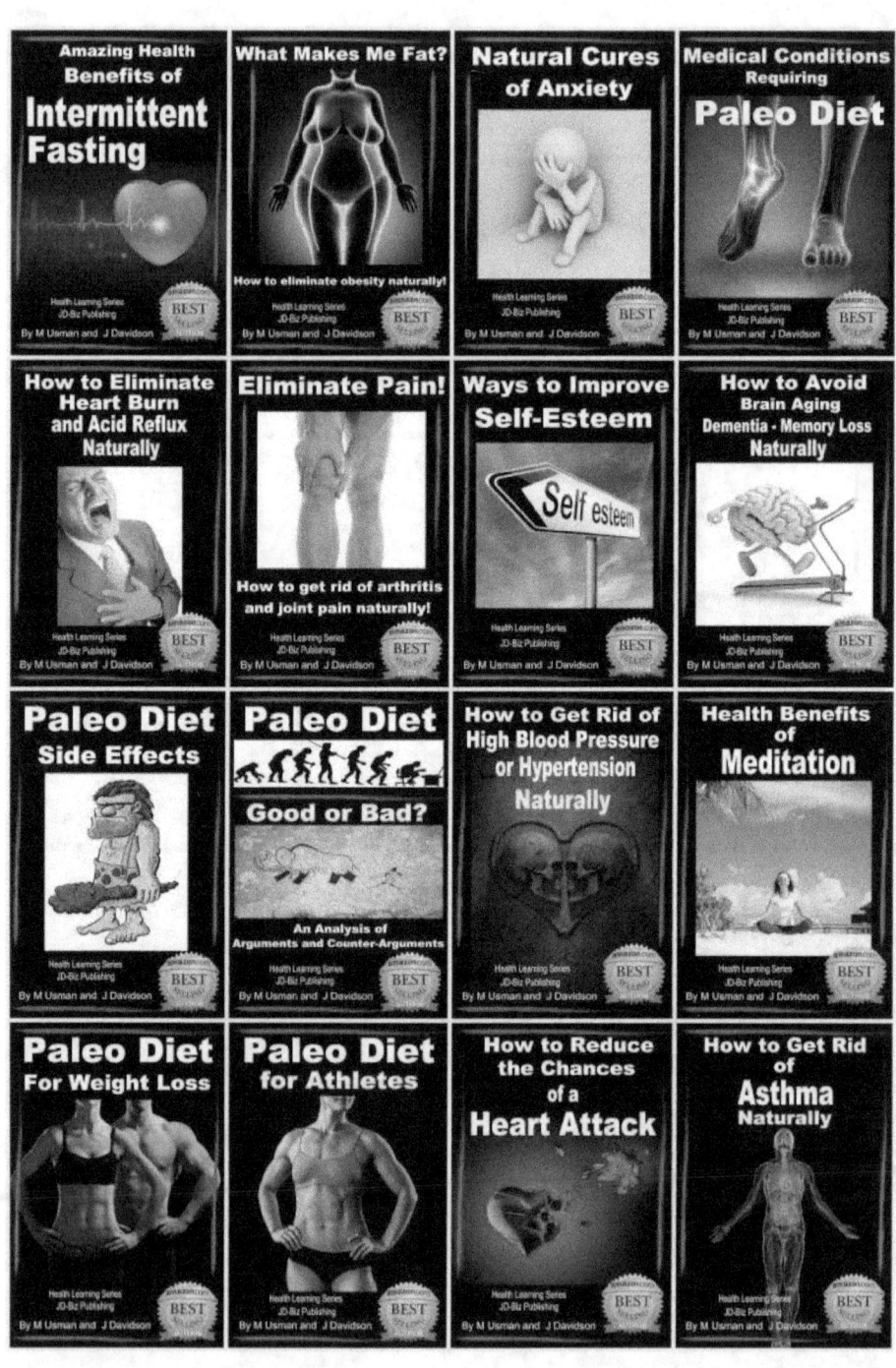

Amazing Animal Book Series

Learn To Draw Series

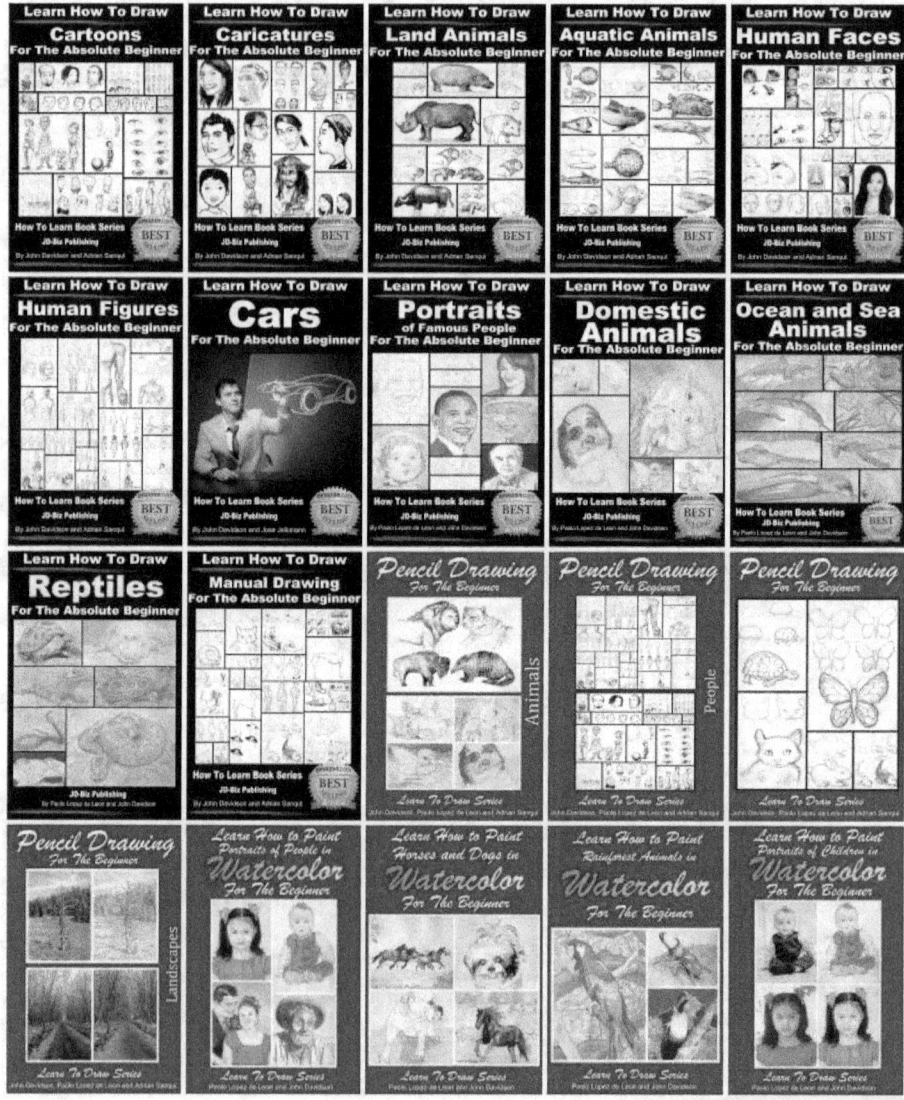

How to Build and Plan Books

Entrepreneur Book Series

PUBLISHER

JD-Biz Corp

P O Box 374

Mendon, Utah 84325

http://www.jd-biz.com/